SUPERMARKET
Rules!

SUPERMARKET
Rules!

52 ways to achieve supermarket success

by **HAROLD C. LLOYD**
illustrated by **STEVE HICKNER**

BRIGANTINE MEDIA

Illustrations by Steve Hickner

Brigantine Media
211 North Avenue, St. Johnsbury, Vermont 05819
Phone: 802-751-8802 | Fax: 802-751-8804
Email: neil@brigantinemedia.com
Website: www.brigantinemedia.com

ISBN 978-1-9384064-3-0
Printed in Canada

Dedication

This book is proudly dedicated to the memory of Carol L. Christison. All great people have the ability to positively influence everyone they meet. Carol was just such a person. She challenged me to deliver a meaningful message each year for twenty consecutive years at her industry-renowned convention for the International Dairy-Deli-Bakery Association. I was honored each year to receive Carol's phone call inviting me back to join a speaking roster that included US Presidents, notable chefs, top comedians, world leaders, and famous athletes. She demanded precision and excellence in a way that motivated everyone. I am convinced that through my twenty years of professional association with Carol I grew way beyond my innate potential.

I will always love and be grateful to my mentor and friend, Carol L. Christison.

The Rules

PART THREE: MANAGEMENT

This book contains the fifty-two most relevant rules anyone fortunate enough to be in the supermarket retail business should know. Utilizing these rules will generate more sales, reduce shrink, and most importantly, help build the store team of your dreams.

Developed from "on the floor" experience and through full access to some of the best retailers in the world, these rules range from "very basic" all the way to "never would have thought of that." The bottom line: they all have been time-tested and proven effective. I hope they stimulate much thought and motivate you to grow your business, your people, and yourself.

PART ONE
Merchandising

Make a great first impression.

"THERE'S NO SECOND chance to make a first impression."

Outside your store—your parking lot, lights, landscaping, and outdoor sales area—is where customers form their very first impression.

Make those areas the best they can be. Keep the lot clean, the paint fresh, the lights bright, and the shrubbery mulched. That's the minimum.

Use your outdoor space to reinforce your strategic points of difference. If it's "competitive prices," install an impressive marquee with a changeable message board to convey your positive price image. Walgreens relies heavily on this effective marketing tool. If your store focuses on "fresh," reflect that outside. Complete your lush landscaping earlier than the competition and maintain it better.

Your sale space outside your front door also contributes to the first impression. Restrict the number of different items for sale to six or less for the greatest impact. Make a bold statement with big piles or pallets of product and large signs or a banner. And let customers know how to pay for the products that are outside the store.

Keep outdoor signage to a minimum, and always keep it positive. Use friendly phrases like "Thank you for . . ." and "Please do not . . . ."

Draw customers inside the store by focusing on the outside first!

Manage your "presto area."

WHAT'S THE "PRESTO area"? It's the twenty-foot arc radiating into your store from the front door—basically, the first few steps into your store.

Why is it called the "presto area"? You have the chance to make magic here. Surprise customers, wow them, make their eyes open wide as they enter your store.

How do you do this? In the presto area, have one focal display that supports one of your key strategic points of difference.

- If "being the freshest" is one of your points of difference, a huge display of seasonal flowers, just-baked doughnuts, or juicy cut watermelons on ice will enhance your image.

- If "having the greatest variety" is your trademark, a new item showcase in the presto area will add excitement.

- If your image is based on promotional excitement, support it with a huge "Buy 3 get 1 free" display in the presto area.

Macey's in Utah always impresses customers in the presto area with its promotionally exciting displays. Mountains of competitively priced Halloween candy or piles of strawberries and all the fixin's for scrumptious shortcake instantly grab their customers' eyes and imaginations.

Be a supermarket magician! Take advantage of your presto area.

Scents impact cents.

THE POWER OF the pleasant scent of food is clearly demonstrated in a movie theater. The aroma of fresh-popped popcorn overwhelms our common sense, and we spend twenty dollars or more on fifty cents worth of popcorn and a couple of soft drinks.

This works in the supermarket, too. Enhance the shopping experience in your store with the fabulous scents of food. A meat smoker positioned outside the front door introduces a delicious barbeque aroma. The smell of freshly brewed coffee stimulates the desire to buy a box of K-Cups. No one can resist the smell of just-baked bread—yum!

Shop Rite in South Africa puts its cooking station right at the entrance of the store so customers can sample the great food that they smell as soon as they walk in.

A recent study showed that the scent of oranges increased customers' spend by twenty percent. Wonderful aromas can make customers succumb to unanticipated purchases. Use scents generated in your store to encourage customers to buy.

And take a cue from the movie theater. Put a popcorn machine by register 1 or the customer service desk, and offer customers a cup of popcorn as they enter or check out. You'll give them a great first or last impression.

Raise a glass to longer store visits.

WHAT DO WE see in many hotel lobbies today? A large, attractive urn of ice-cold water with floating slices of lemons, limes, or oranges. Offering a cool drink makes their guests feel welcome and refreshed. It's the same thing you do when a guest comes to your home.

Try this same idea in your store to welcome customers. Informal research has shown that offering customers a beverage early in their shopping experience encourages them to stay longer. What's great

about that? For every extra minute a customer stays in your store, she spends approximately two dollars more.

The Fresh Street Market in Vancouver leads off their store with the produce department. In the center of the department is a colorfully garnished urn full of water, ice, and fruit slices. It's an inexpensive way to convey freshness and friendliness, and maximize sales.

A toast to longer store visits!

Keep it fresh.

FRESH FOOD CASES can be a major attraction in your store. Or they can be a major turn-off. It all depends on how you take care of them.

In the seafood department: the old ice must be completely removed everyday and replaced with fresh ice. If not, the case will give off that "fishy smell." There's no avoiding this chore.

Now, let's talk about garnish. Nothing works better to grab the customer's eye in a seafood or deli case than creative and fresh garnish. Your employees don't need to have an art degree to learn to garnish well. There are plenty of three- and four-step "how to garnish" instructional videos available online. Use distressed produce that has removable blemishes.

Get rid of the plastic vines and grapes, please. You're promoting "fresh" in these cases!

And one more must-do in your deli case: no utensils. For years, the rule has been to place all spoons, ladles, and tongs in the same corner of the bowl and in the same direction. It's pleasing to the eye and minimizes clutter. But it is far less sanitary than using a fresh spoon each time. In the Whole Foods in Virginia Beach, Virginia, there are no utensils in the case. Instead, they are stored, sanitized, and air-dried in a container behind the deli case. Each transaction gets a clean utensil. No cross-contamination from a handle on a utensil accidentally touching some product in an adjacent bowl.

Fresh ice, fresh garnish, fresh utensils. Keep it fresh!

Follow the rule of six.

IF YOU CAN'T afford to make or stock at least six of a particular item, don't have it at all.

No one buys the last bag of cookies or loaf of bread. Customers ask themselves, "Why is it the last? Is it stale? Out of code? A broken package?"

You may think you're providing great service by giving one or two customers what they want. But a few of everything to please everyone leads to a confusing display and tons of shrink.

Before discontinuing an item you've sold for years that has dwindled down to only two or three sales a day, develop a thirty-day resurrection plan. Try to grow sales of that item back to at least six a day. If you haven't increased sales of the item to your goal level in thirty days, give it the axe.

Sampling sells!

WHY DO PUBLIX, HEB, Hy-Vee, and Schnucks have a dedicated sampling kiosk in each store staffed for over forty hours each week? Why does every Costco have three or four sampling stations staffed almost all the time? Sampling sells products.

Customers love sampling. In fact, if you ask Costco customers why they are so loyal to the store, product sampling is one of their top four responses. Sampling is supermarket theater.

I'm not talking about an elderly lady wearing a hair net, positioned behind a wobbly card table with a soiled tablecloth, handing out cheese chunks with toothpicks to kids who have wandered away from Mom.

Check HEB's Showtime endcaps or Publix's Aprons program to see sampling done right. They never sample just one item. They prepare a meal. Offer samples of an entire meal, and the odds of a sale of at least one of those items skyrocket.

Save Mart Supermarkets in California takes a more informal approach. The stores don't have dedicated stations, but instead, use sampling in a spontaneous, versatile way. The stores often promote seasonal items, setting up sampling demos in a matter of minutes for a couple of hours.

The shopper who is engaged by sampling will spend ten to twenty percent more money than one who isn't. As the customer approaches the sampling table, she slows down, then stops to think about the items being sampled and related purchases.

It is this extra minute or two in your store that adds to the customer's register tape. Sampling is an investment with a positive return. The best retailers know this.

Make special orders special.

MEAT, SEAFOOD, DELI, bakery, and produce departments can all build great customer connections through special orders. Making a wedding cake, veggie tray, or crown roast is a special service that customers appreciate and remember.

Make special orders a specialty of your store.

Create a "Special Orders" sign that works as a billboard to attract more special orders:

- Title the eight-by-two-foot sign: "Special Orders for Special Customers."

- Illuminate the sign with LED lights.

- Hang seven bright-colored clipboards on the

sign, marked for each day of the week. That's where your special orders will be posted.

- Create a "Special Orders" sign for each department that does special orders and make sure customers can see it clearly.

Cross-train everyone in the department to accurately take special orders on the phone and face-to-face. Keep the appropriate forms near the phone with a clean space to work.

And when the order is ready, attach the creator's business card and one helium balloon to the special order. Everyone will see the customer walking out of the store with the special order.

Make it really special!

Use a party planner.

AND ON THE subject of special orders, here's another way to make the experience even more special ... and add more sales.

What does a customer do while waiting to pick up a special order? She waits. What could we help her do? Shop for the rest of the items she needs for her party.

Create a "party planner"—a shopping list for special events. It's easy to do. It just needs to be one side of a sheet of paper, with four columns of products: two columns of food items and two columns of non-food items, all party-related. Include aisle locations for each item on the list to make it as easy as possible for the customer to find them.

Hand a "party planner" to every customer when they come to pick up a special order. Instead of waiting for her cake or cheese platter, the customer can use the time to complete her party shopping, with the help of the list.

Don't keep them waiting!

When the wind dies down, row.

MOST OF THE excitement in a supermarket is around the perimeter of the store: deli, bakery, meat, produce, and prepared food. The center store—the grocery department—is usually much less visually interesting. If the wind has died down in this area of your store, my advice is to get out the oars and row. There are plenty of ways to bring customers into your center store aisles.

Blades and perpendicular shelf-talkers promoting new items and temporary savings are attention-grabbers. Floor decals are also great for promoting a store brand or service and help attract customers into the aisle.

HEB in Texas is one of the best at pulling customers up and down the grocery aisles. Its aisles have four-foot promotional sections with endcap-style signage. The stores also attract customers into their aisles by hanging several bright yellow, dollar bill-sized coupons on shower curtain hooks. Customers can't miss seeing the coupons when they glance down the aisles. When they learn how valuable they are, customers start a treasure hunt for more coupons throughout the grocery area.

To create more interest in the center store, try building merchandise vignettes and visual displays in the aisles and on endcaps. Add an operating clothes dryer (with the heating element removed) halfway down the laundry aisle to grab attention.

MDI's Galaxy Food Stores makes its grocery section a local attraction with its hilarious "outhouse" displays at the end of the toilet paper aisle.

Row, row, row your aisles . . . to profitability!

Give your displays the AIDA test.

AIDA—IN SUPERMARKETS, it's the purchase process: Attention/Interest/Desire/Action.

After building a display, step back and give it the AIDA test.

First, does the display capture the customers' **Attention**? Bright helium balloons, a blinking strobe light, a huge stuffed animal—all super attention grabbers.

Second, what gets the customers' **Interest**? "Limited time only," "peak of season," "great source of vitamin C," and "top ten best seller!"

Third, will it trigger a **Desire** in the customer to buy the product? Customers want lots of things—to save money, to buy the freshest product available, to stock up on items they use often, just to name a few.

Make sure your display instantly stimulates at least one of their desires.

Fourth, customers must be motivated to **Action**. Help them complete the transaction. Provide bigger bags and a trash bin for the husks right next to the fabulous display of fresh-picked, local corn on the cob. Offer samples of the latest-and-greatest trendy snack product to entice customers to drop a package in their carts. Bananas in the cereal aisle? It's a no-brainer.

Create signs of success.

PRODUCT SIGNS CAN be much more than conveyors of basic information such as, "What is this?" and "How much does it cost?" Signs can enlighten the customer about the wonders of the product.

Include information on your signs that does at least one of the following:

1. Tells a story: "Made in Florence, Italy, by artisan bakers."

2. Solves a problem: "Great for a quick, nutritious snack."

3. Answers a question: "Fresh, never frozen" or "Limited time only."

Trader Joe's is a wonderful storyteller. Customers are entertained and enlightened by the creative signage throughout their stores. My local Trader Joe's had an endcap with five environmentally friendly cleaning products and an attractive, handmade sign that said, "The Ingredients for a Successful Afternoon of Spring Cleaning." That's a sign that almost makes you *want* to clean!

Beware of decimal creep.

IMPULSE SALES ARE purchases that occur in an instant. Keep the information clear and concise.

I'll give you an example. Merchandising small bouquets of fresh cut flowers near the express lanes at 6:00 p.m. is a good idea. And pricing the bouquets at $5—no decimals—is a great idea.

$4.79 or $5.29 just doesn't provide the clarity and ease that $5 does. The extra time it takes to decide on a purchase allows customers time to change their mind on a discretionary purchase. "Maybe I should take two bouquets . . . What's two times $4.79? Never mind, I shouldn't buy these anyway. I don't need them!"

I did an experiment recently to prove the power of the round number price point. On one half of a table were packages of a dozen cupcakes. On the other side, half sheet cakes. The sign on the cupcakes read $4.49, and the cakes had a sign for $5.49.

The store manager tracked the sales of the two items for a week in two stores. After that, he replaced the two signs with one, larger sign that read, "Your choice: $5."

Result: the sales of the cupcakes and cakes increased by over three hundred percent.

For impulse items, lose the decimals to gain sales.

Showcase signature items.

EVER BEEN INFLUENCED by a restaurant server who was so convincing about how wonderful their signature dish was that you ordered it without even looking at the menu? And when you ate it, you couldn't wait to return for more?

Signature items in your store are powerful magnets. Your employees need to encourage customers to try those signature items to hook customers into returning. How to train them to do it? Here are a couple of ideas.

One: Showcase a different signature item in the break room each month so all the employees taste it and comment. When they know how good it is, they'll recommend it to customers.

Two: At the end of their first month on the job, give new employees a goodie bag that has six store brand and signature items in it. This serves two purposes: it's a mini-award for the employee's first month of work, and it exposes them to signature items they can recommend to customers.

Concord Markets in Toronto, Canada, rewards employees after their first week on the job with a shopping bag full of signature goodies. It's a great way to make sure everyone who works in the store knows the special items that Concord Markets sells.

Support your brand.

IT'S A FACT that store brands (aka private labels) return higher margin dollars per unit than national brands. Store brands are exclusive to you and can be a powerful point of difference.

The Kroger Company is an industry leader in its commitment to its store brands. Some of its stores allocate more than half of their end displays to store brands. Kroger cross-merchandises its store brands very effectively. Its power panels and shelf extenders promote store brand items most of the time.

The average retailer's store brand sales make up seventeen percent of its total sales, but the best retailers earn over twenty-five percent of sales from store brands.

Support your store brand—it will give you both exclusive products and greater margins.

Keep your customers rolling in the aisles.

AT A STORE'S grand opening, the aisles are wide and unobstructed. Store designers know how wide aisles must be to handle the traffic they hope to attract. But over time, the aisle stacks, wings, shippers, pallets, and table displays begin to narrow your aisles.

Don't give in to product creep in your aisles! Keep them wide so customers can navigate easily.

All main perimeter aisles should be at least nine feet wide. Aisles separating departments (primary aisles) should be at least seven feet wide. And aisles within the departments and everywhere else (secondary aisles) should be at least five feet wide.

Since a standard shopping cart is about twenty-four inches wide, two carts passing comfortably in an aisle require almost five feet. A two-by-two foot shipper display in a five-foot aisle creates an instant bottleneck. A four-foot table display turns a primary aisle into an obstacle course. A nine-foot perimeter aisle becomes gridlocked on a busy day when a four-foot pallet drop is added.

Most customers detest a congested store. I find it interesting that the most common customer compliment during a grand re-opening is, "the aisles in this store are now so nice and wide and easy to shop!" when, in fact, the aisle widths were never changed. The "carton creep" and "aisle insanity" were just eliminated with the store redesign.

Maintain minimum aisle widths as a customer convenience. After all, they can't buy it if they can't get to it!

Up and at 'em!

SOME STATES OUTLAW product on the floor. All managers should outlaw it in their stores.

Display merchandise up and off the floor. It doesn't matter if the product is protected by cardboard or shrink-wrap. Keep it off the floor.

Focus groups of customers say they are disgusted to think that product that they bring into their homes may have spent some time on the floor in a grocery store.

It's so easy to raise products off the floor, it's amazing that anyone still breaks this rule. Put a base under the endcap display. It will help in several ways:

- A base or pallet adds at least six inches to the height of a display, putting more of the product where customers can easily see it.

- Customers push shopping carts close to displays when rounding a corner. There will be less damage to merchandise when it doesn't rest directly on the floor.

- When merchandise is left on the floor for a while, floor wax seeps under it and adheres it to the floor, requiring a lot of elbow grease to remove. This won't happen when merchandise rests on a base instead of directly on the floor.

It's simple—keep products up and at 'em and off the floor.

Make the last impression a lasting one.

THE SHOPPING EXPERIENCE is not over when the cashier takes the customer's payment and the bags are loaded in the cart.

Much more happens. On the way to the exit, the customer walks past broken bags of dog food and rock salt, the unmanaged Rug Doctor® display, nearly empty gumball machines, local magazines, and vending machines with "Out of Order" signs affixed with tape.

That's no way to leave a final impression of your store.

Don't ignore what the customers see in their final steps inside your store and in the parking lot. Unfriendly signage, disheveled displays, and litter make customers think you don't care.

Make sure everything the customer sees at the exit contributes to the positive impression you've created throughout the store. Wegman's speaks to their freshness, their heritage, the multitude of services they offer, and their penchant for superior customer service in the customer's final steps as they exit their fabulous stores.

We usually remember the last thing we see—so make it good!

PART TWO

Operations

Welcome customers with name tags.

THE MOST BASIC of all customer relations tools is the name tag. When the customer and employee connect by name, a relationship begins. Make sure your associates' name tags make customers feel welcome.

Name tag basics:

- Use the first name only.
- The font must be easy to read and contrast with the tag's background.
- The name must be readable from at least twenty feet away.

- Wear the name tag on the right side of the shirt or apron for maximum exposure. When two people shake hands, the name tag will be fully exposed.

- Replace name tags every one to two years before they get faded or chipped.

It's fun to add a little more to the name tag to encourage engagement between employees and customers. Have associates choose one or more of the following options on their name tags (in smaller print under their name):

1. Hometown
2. Years of service or starting year with the company
3. High school and graduating year
4. Response to the words, "Ask me about ..."

The Sweetbay chain of supermarkets (now part of Bi-Lo and rebranded as Winn-Dixie) put "Ask me about ..." on their name tags. Employees completed the phrase many different ways: "Ask me about ... my three sons;" "Ask me about ... crossword puzzles;" "Ask me about ... scuba diving."

Think of the name tag as a welcome mat. You want it to make a great first impression!

The eight-foot rule.

HELP EMPLOYEES ENGAGE with customers with the eight-foot rule.

It's a simple idea: your employees greet every customer who walks within eight feet of them. That's it!

First, employees need to be able to estimate the distance. Overwaitea Foods in Canada has a clever solution. They preach a ten-foot rule. Each store highlights its ten-foot policy with a big blue ten-foot-long strip of tape on the floor in the hallway leading to the break room. The tape reminds employees several times a day about the rule and what ten feet looks like.

Second, what should the employee say to the customer? "How are you?" just doesn't make the grade.

Try one of these:

- "Let me know if I can help you in any way."
- "Thanks for shopping with us today."
- "We appreciate your business."

Any of these greetings is appropriate and polite, and can open a conversation between an employee and a customer that can lead to sales.

I'd like to see the eight-foot rule applied not only to interactions between store personnel and customers, but also between managers and employees. Managers should model the eight-foot rule, remembering to greet every employee who comes within eight feet with a hearty "Good Morning!" or "Your department looks great!"

The eight-foot rule can help make your store a friendlier place to shop and a more enjoyable place to work, too.

Encourage shopping lists.

I HAVE ASKED many retailers if a customer who shops with a shopping list buys more or less than a customer without one. Almost every retailer says, "less." They think that customers restrict themselves to purchasing *only* what is on the list.

That's not true! People make lists so they won't forget what they need to buy. If you're a good merchandiser, customers who have shopping lists will be just as likely to buy additional items as anyone.

Let's do the numbers. The average item in a supermarket retails for about $2.50. The average total order is $25. So one item typically represents ten percent of an order. If a non-list maker forgets two items while shopping, he will end up buying twenty percent less than a list maker who buys everything on a list. In fact, three different studies show that people who shop with a shopping list (paper or a smartphone app) buy between eleven and twenty-one percent more.

Encourage the use of shopping lists. Display your ads (a form of a shopping list) prominently in the "presto area" (Rule 13). Give customers printed shopping lists with products arranged alphabetically, and include their aisle locations.

Super 1 Foods of Montana, Idaho, and Washington gives customers a shopping list printed lengthwise on the outside of an envelope, so a customer can make a list and keep coupons inside. That idea might make *all* their customers list makers!

Don't sell what you wouldn't buy.

THE GOLDEN RULE of supermarkets might go like this: "If you wouldn't buy it for your family, don't sell it to your customers."

This means:

- Don't re-grind fresh ground beef with older product to move it out.

- Don't re-date a dozen containers of cut veggies because they still look good enough to sell.

- Don't stir that potato salad for the third time to remove the brown hue forming on the surface.

This rule is very basic and very profound. It is a policy that builds a strong culture.

Display this rule in break rooms and in all the prep areas as a constant reminder. If customers see it, all the better. "If you wouldn't buy it for your family, don't sell it to your customers."

We learned it as children . . . the Golden Rule is always the best approach.

Open registers on each end first.

WHENEVER TWO OR more registers are needed, keep the registers at each end of your line open. The first register you open should be the one on the end closest to the front entrance. The second one you open should be at the other end of the registers, close to your exit doors. Then open the registers in the middle of the line-up as you need them.

Here's why . . . if a cashier is positioned at the register by the entrance door, he/she can be a greeter while serving as a cashier. It's easy enough for the cashier to say "good morning" to a customer entering the store while processing an order for another shopper.

The cashier at the other end, near the exit doors, can watch for shoplifters. When a shoplifter attempts to exit the store, he/she is forced to go around the bank of registers because each lane is typically blocked off in some way. By positioning a cashier at the far end, you have a "sentry" guarding the exit as a deterrent.

I often see two cashiers positioned side by side on, say, registers 3 and 4 in a seven-register line-up. It might be because those registers are under the heater that works best or the fatigue mats at those registers are the most comfortable. Don't make this mistake!

And one more problem with cashiers next to each other: the cashiers are more likely to socialize with each other when their registers are in close proximity. When that happens, customers might not be given the attention they deserve.

You may be surprised how much this simple rule adds to your bottom line.

Shopping cart and hand basket basics.

A CUSTOMER PUSHING a shopping cart will buy more than a customer shopping with a hand basket—200 percent more. But many customers decide on impulse which one they'll grab. You can influence their choice.

Place shopping carts in three locations:

- Outside—For customers who want to enter the store with a cart, maybe to help carry a child.

- In the foyer—For customers who don't like

taking a cart that might be wet or dusty.

- In the back center of the store (typically the meat aisle)—For customers who didn't think they needed a cart at the entrance, but are picking up more than they anticipated. This cart corral needs only ten or twelve carts.

Always have at least one big or bulky item for sale in the front of the store "piled high and priced to fly!" An eight-pack of paper towels, a 24-pack of soda, or a bin of ripe watermelons will tempt customers, and they'll need a cart to transport them.

Don't place a stack of hand baskets in the foyer. Never tempt customers to trade down their capacity to buy. Some customers will opt for the hand basket, and now you have lost half the customer's buying potential.

Instead, place the first stack of hand baskets twenty feet away from the front doors, next to the in-store flyer rack in the center of the main aisle.

The second, third, fourth, fifth, and yes, the sixth stacks of hand baskets go next to the rotisserie chicken display, the salad bar, the gallon milk section, by the service deli, and near the entrance to the greeting card aisle.

If you have a pharmacy, place a seventh stack behind the counter. Offer customers their filled prescription in a hand basket if they come to the pick-up window without a cart or basket. It's great suggestive selling without saying a word.

Give customers plenty of carts and hand baskets to carry your products to the cash register!

Don't slip!

WATER ON THE floor is common in the supermarket work environment. Food prep, broken or leaky packaging, and the weather all contribute to wet floors. Be careful! Dangerous and expensive slip-and-falls may happen when floors are wet.

Require your employees to wear slip-resistant footwear. It's standard gear in virtually every restaurant, and I think it should be the same in supermarkets, especially where food preparation is taking place.

The average slip-and-fall injury costs a company over $8,000. You want to protect your employees' safety as well as protect your company against financial loss.

Some retailers pay for the specialized footwear. Others offer discounts and repayment plans.

As they say in the restaurant industry, "if you're working, you're wearing (slip-resistant footwear)."

Face upstream.

DID YOU KNOW there is a right and wrong direction to face when working in an aisle? You should face "upstream."

Customers flow through the aisles in both directions, but a majority of customers do shop in one direction. All employees working in an aisle should be positioned next to their workstation or cart so they are facing the direction that the majority of customers move; facing "upstream," against the flow of customers.

The reason for this is simple. Facing customers while working is like putting out a welcome mat, as if to say, "ask me a question." Facing "downstream" is like telling the customer you are too busy to be bothered. Customers are far more likely to ask a question

of a clerk who is facing them than one whose back is toward them.

Special note: Admittedly, facing upstream can be less productive. Associates won't be able to put up as much stock if they are frequently answering questions or suggestively selling. So the exception to the "face upstream" rule is at a warehouse store or deep-discount format store where customer service is optional and productivity is paramount.

Hair and food don't mix.

EVER FIND A hair in your food at a restaurant? Ninety percent of people I've asked said they have. And when I ask, "Have you ever gone back to that restaurant?" most say "no."

People hate to find a stray hair in their food. But some managers in supermarkets still allow their employees to work around open food without any type of hair restraint. Because local ordinances do not always require hairnets or hats for food workers, some managers think that it's not necessary.

Don't make this mistake. Never allow an employee or vendor near unpackaged food without complete hair restraint. The average person loses fifty to seventy hairs per day.

The most complete policy I've seen to date was at a Pak 'n Save in New Zealand. There was a bold sign posted by every entrance to the food preparation areas that read: "Do not cross this line without a hair restraint, proper attire, and a Food Safety Certification." This straightforward statement succinctly addressed the issue.

Like many health and cleanliness concerns in the supermarket industry, keeping hair out of food is a small matter with large consequences.

Take care of business.

HERE'S A FUN idea that will energize your employees, entertain your customers, and spruce up the look of your store—in less than five minutes!

Try taking care of business. At 11:00 a.m., 4:00 p.m., and 7:00 p.m., play the 1970s Bachman-Turner Overdrive song "Takin' Care of Business" *loudly* over the intercom. As soon as they hear the song start, all employees not directly assisting a customer will come out onto the sales floor and sweep, freshen, primp, fill, and straighten anything that needs it.

That means *every* employee—managers included! With everyone's cooperation, the entire store will look refreshed, or a least more presentable, in just a few minutes.

And customers will love to see everyone in the store "takin' care of business!"

Harps Foods in Arkansas lives by this rule. The company even had the song rewritten by one of the original artists to include the name "Harps" in the lyrics.

Trash the trash.

EVERY RETAILER KNOWS the importance of a clean store. To some, that means having trash receptacles at every turn. But I think the number of trash cans should be *minimized* in a supermarket. Put them near sampling stations and at the exit door, and that's all.

I'll explain my dislike of trash cans.

- Trash cans are not at all attractive.

- Trash cans don't promote selling, but instead, take up valuable display space.

- Trash cans are a trip hazard.

- Trash cans are often used by shoplifters to dispose of pilfered product's packaging.

What trash is generated in a supermarket? Cardboard, plastic wrap? Sure, but that should be taken to the back, not crammed in store receptacles. Customers sometimes want to get rid of a used tissue or old shopping list. These items can be disposed of in the trash can at the exit.

And one more thing about trash cans: *never* use black or green trash can liners—only clear ones. Dishonest employees can use solid trash can liners to remove merchandise from the store by concealing it as trash, taking it out back, and collecting it later.

Clear plastic bags allow you to see through the bag. Managers can see what's going out in the trash and can check if it can be reclaimed in some way. Damaged or out-of-date merchandise may look like garbage to an employee, but often it can be credited or salvaged by a vendor or wholesaler.

Throw out your old ideas about trash!

Keep your restrooms clean.

THIS SOUNDS LIKE a rule you don't need to hear. Anyone in charge of operating a supermarket has clean restrooms high on the to-do list. But it's far more important than you may think.

To the customer, clean restrooms are one of the top three most accurate indicators of a clean store. (The other two are the condition of the store's front entrance and the condition of your employees' uniforms.)

And this doesn't just apply to the public restrooms. Keep your staff restrooms spotless, too. They send a clear message to your employees that you care about them.

To achieve clean restrooms, many operators rely on a checklist posted on the back of the washroom door. It's initialed every hour by an employee inspector. But a mess could occur just minutes after an inspection. Have an additional line of defense.

Here's a great idea I saw in a roadside restaurant somewhere in North Carolina. In the restroom, six feet off the floor near the door was a light switch with a small sign that read, "If this restroom is not perfectly clean, please flip this switch." Turns out, when the switch was flipped, a light was activated in the manager's office, who could respond immediately.

In your supermarket, the light should be hooked up somewhere in the store where a responsible person will be sure to see—maybe a light at your customer service desk, since that's always staffed.

PS: Add a small bouquet of flowers on the sink in each restroom. The flowers will last a week and give your restrooms an extra-pleasant image.

Don't be embarrassed by your back room.

MORE PEOPLE SEE your back room area than you might think. Vendors go into the back regularly. Customers often venture back there looking for the restrooms.

Your back room should be a source of pride, not of shame.

An embarrassing back room usually begins with ugly, dented, stickered, and crooked double doors. The floors are dirty and tiles are missing. Parts of the back room don't smell good. An embarrassing back room leaves employees and guests with the impression that the store isn't well managed. And they will tell other people what they have seen in your embarrassing back room.

Care about your back room. Try these ideas:

- Include the back room on every manager's store walk. You'll be sure everything is kept clean if you're inspecting this area regularly.

- Reword all your back room signs so they are positive and professional. Remember, outsiders are viewing these messages.

- Have your back room doors "skinned" with attractive graphics representing the departments where they are located. A huge gallon of milk displayed across the double doors leading to the dairy cooler in the back will make a great impression.

- Budget to remodel your back room when you remodel your store.

The back room is an important part of the store. Be proud for anyone to see it.

Enforce a No-Fly Zone.

MANAGING THE RECEIVING area is critical to tracking your inventory. If you receive less than you're billed for, your profit margins shrink. And while a customer may steal one item, a vendor can take cases of goods. Direct store delivery vendors often have access in and out of the store in less-than-secure conditions.

Create a No-Fly Zone at your receiving area—a fifteen-foot arc or rectangle coming directly from the main receiving door. Stripe the No-Fly Zone with red or yellow paint, just like a no parking area in a parking lot.

Set the rule for all deliveries: all vendors entering or leaving the store through the receiving door must pass across the No-Fly Zone. When they do, they must stop and wait for an authorized store employee to check that what they are bringing in or taking out is authorized and documented. Make your No-Fly Zone policy clear with signage on the wall outside the receiving area and a letter to all vendors that outline the rules. Any vendor who doesn't stop in the No-Fly Zone may be asked to forfeit the product because you can't be certain it wasn't taken off your shelves.

No flying through the receiving area without being scrutinized.

Secure your compactor door.

YOU'RE CAREFUL ABOUT the front doors to your store, with cameras, greeters, and plenty of monitoring to make sure they are safe and secure. But what about your back doors?

Specifically, I'm talking about your compactor door. Most stores have a metal double door mounted on the outside wall in the back room. This door opens up to a chute that extends from the outside wall into an opening in a compactor unit that compacts and contains the store's garbage until it is hauled away.

In most states there are laws dictating the minimum age of anyone using a compactor. Store management should also strictly control the use of these machines.

Once upon a time, I wondered if employees and vendors, who had access to the compactor, might be improperly disposing of product. So I followed our thirty-yarder as it was being hauled to the municipal dump to see if that was true.

Unfortunately, my theory played out all too well. I found a case of spaghetti sauce with only a few broken jars, a complete roll of shrink film from the meat department, a half case of lettuce, and six cases of 7-Up. It was impossible to trace these items back to the person who threw them away to discover why they had been discarded. But I learned that there was far too much access to our compactor door.

Regulate access to your compactor door with:

- A lock that store management controls, and a strict procedure for unlocking the compactor door only at predetermined times.

- A camera mounted so the face of anyone opening the compactor door will be clearly visible along with whatever they are discarding.

- Bold signage about the importance of exercising care in discarding product, noting that the compactor door area is under electronic surveillance twenty-four hours a day.

Don't let your store's assets get thrown away!

Track the traffic.

UNDERSTAND THE FLOW of customer traf-
fic around your store. Sales are crimped when the
shopper can't get to the items they want. Conduct a
customer traffic study.

What if you discovered that 63 out of 100 customers who enter your store travel down aisle four, but
aisle seven gets only 18 percent of all store customers?
You would look at resetting aisle seven, or making
sure the aisle opening isn't restricted by something. If
you found that 70 percent of customers came to the
produce department through a less desirable secondary entrance, you would reset the opening to redirect
the customers into the department so they don't miss

the highly profitable fresh-cut fruit section.

Traffic studies are done by major retailers using GPS and elaborate computer systems, and they cost tens of thousands of dollars. But traffic studies can be done on a small budget, too.

Hire a few local college interns for a week. Their job is to clandestinely follow 150 to 200 customers in the morning, afternoon, and evening for seven days, tracking their every move on a map of the store. If the customer is pushing a cart, the observer makes a solid line representing the customer's path. If she leaves the cart to go after an item, that path is depicted with a dotted line. If the customer picks up an item and puts it in her cart, a solid dot is placed where the item was selected. If the customer picks up an item and puts it back down, a open dot is recorded.

Dotted lines typically identify a traffic jam. Open dots represent a rejected item. There's a lot to evaluate from this data.

Conduct a traffic study in your store at least every five years and after every major remodel of the store or an individual department.

Track your store's traffic. You'll learn more than you might expect.

Hire Bob, Mitch, and Lisa.

ACCIDENTAL OR INTENTIONAL, product that leaves the store without being paid for is shrink that must be minimized. That's why you need to hire Bob, Mitch, and Lisa.

Your cashiers are your last line of defense. They must make sure that an eight-pack of paper towels under the cart gets scanned and a small spice bottle isn't forgotten under a baby blanket in the child's seat. But how does a manager help cashiers remember to check every customer? That's where your new hires—Bob, Mitch, and Lisa—come in.

When the manager notices a bag of dog food on the bottom of a customer's cart, he/she should ask the cashier, "Have you seen BOB this morning?" The cashier would answer "yes" or "no," and check for an item at the **B**ottom **O**f the **B**asket.

When the manager sees a customer reading a magazine, ask, "Did you see MITCH?" The cashier would be alerted to look for unpaid **M**erchandise **I**n **T**he **C**ustomer's **H**and.

And if the manager saw the spice jar in the baby's blanket? Ask the cashier if she saw LISA—she'll remember to look for an item **L**eft **I**n the **S**eating **A**rea.

Customers won't know you're checking up on them, and cashiers will be reminded of a really important responsibility.

Farm Fresh in Virginia Beach, Virginia, uses this system. The store manager uses the "code names" to communicate with the front-end staff to ensure that products are checked out properly.

Beat the waiting game.

CUSTOMERS HATE TO wait in line at the super-market. In an Ipsos Public Affairs survey in 2006, supermarkets were named as the most frustrating place to wait, and mentioned more often than the Department of Motor Vehicles and the doctor's office combined.

Everyone who works in supermarkets knows there is an optimal time to add more registers to minimize line wait. But when?

Start by defining your store's standard for check-out line wait. Traditionally, an acceptable line length is four customers—"four, no more!" A more gener-ous policy is "two, then you." Rouse's Supermarkets in Louisiana has a "you're next!" policy that opens a new line if more than one person is waiting. Decide what works for your store, and then communicate your policy to all your employees. Develop a plan for adding cashiers at whatever line length you choose.

Add a "fire drill" plan for when the lines begin to back up. When they're needed, make an announcement recruiting the pre-determined employees in the store who have been cross-trained to bag groceries or run a register. In an instant, those employees should drop what they're doing and take a position on the front lines. The fire drill should last only a few minutes with the infusion of four or five additional helpers. Your customers will be amazed by your responsiveness.

It's not over 'til it's over.

WHAT KIND OF feeling do you get when you walk by a store in the mall that has its security gates pulled halfway down? Or when a restaurant shuts off some of the lights while you are eating a late dinner? Unwelcomed.

Customers who shop late feel the same way when you turn off lights or close some service areas later in the evening. They get the message that even though your store is open until midnight, you really don't expect them to shop there after eight. And if you don't make them feel welcome, they won't.

If you're open late, look alive, not ready to close. Keep all the lights on in prep areas until closing, even if there are no employees on duty. Leave instructions on how customers can get assistance if they need something not available in the case. When the lights are bright throughout the store, customers feel safe and welcome when they shop at night.

Plenty of customers shop late after the kids have gone to bed or when their work shift is over. Make their shopping experience as complete as the one customers in the daytime enjoy!

PART THREE

Management

What's in your pockets?

GREAT STORE MANAGERS work an average of 52 hours per week. They spend 80 to 90 percent of their time walking the store.

Travel lightly but always have these essentials in your pockets:

1. *Three business cards.* Three's enough because "reloading" is just a quick run back to the office. Give them out to customers when you introduce yourself.

2. *Ten one-dollar bills.* In case a customer lost some money in a vending machine or couldn't wait in line to return an item to customer service. Remove the hassle of the refund with a little pocket money.

3. *Small notepad and pen.* Use these to

document an incident or write down a customer's name and contact information.

4. *Box cutter.* For trimming a protruding piece of cardboard or removing a dated sign.

5. *Small roll of Scotch® tape.* It's handy when a can is losing its label. (If a $1 can of beans ends up without a label, it goes in the reclaim box—a loss that requires $100 in sales to cover.)

6. *Smartphone or small camera.* Ideal for photographing a great sign or display to show at your next department managers' meeting. Also for documenting a slip-and-fall site.

7. *Ten pennies.* Start your day with ten pennies in your left-hand pocket. As you go through your day, give sincere praise to people who deserve it, and move a penny to the other pocket each time you do. For example, tell your maintenance guy that the outside of the store looks great. Move a penny to your right-hand pocket. Tell a customer that the steaks she selected were an excellent choice. Move a penny. At the end of the day, count the pennies remaining in your left hand pocket. There shouldn't be any.

Oh yes, one more thing. Pack the mints.

Huddle up!

TARGET, ONE OF the most successful retailers in the US, includes in its Standard Operating Procedures manual that each store must conduct three huddles per day. Most supermarkets don't do them at all.

I recommend two huddles each day. A huddle is an informal, ten-minute (set a timer) meeting. One person from each department (a manager or an associate) participates in the huddle. They stand in a circle in the middle of the store. Each person in the huddle has one minute or less to share an idea, voice a concern, or give information involving that day's business. Huddles can be used to introduce a new item, request to borrow someone's pallet jack,

or announce that the front end had two call-outs and there might be a need to borrow baggers at the noon rush.

Schnucks, headquartered in St. Louis, Missouri, does two ten-minute huddles each day with its managers and employees.

Have a huddle just before the doors open in the morning to bring the team together to kick off the day. Start off the late shift with an evening huddle. Include at least one participant from the day shift in the evening huddle to alert everyone to some of the challenges they may experience that evening, such as an out-of-stock item or a shortage of help.

Two huddles every day foster team communication and cooperation.

Log your refunds.

YOU KNOW YOU get lots of information from customer complaints. That's why the best supermarket operators encourage customer comments and suggestions. But another great source of information is from your refund log.

Every supermarket gets returns and has to refund customers' money. Be sure to keep track of all refunds given. Then monitor that refund log regularly. Look for patterns and recurring issues in your database of items that have been returned to the store. Four gallons of milk returned in the same week could indicate a vendor issue or a receiving malfunction. Three sheet cakes returned in a month is cause for concern in your bakery.

Brown's Shop Rite in the Delaware Valley pays close attention to all refunds and follows up with any negative trends they uncover.

A refund log must be created and routinely analyzed. It's an early warning system for bigger issues.

Apply Parkinson's Law.

CYRIL NORTHCOTE PARKINSON first wrote his law in the *Economist* in 1955: "Work expands to fill the time available for its completion." Use Parkinson's Law as a guide to the way a manager should assign a task.

Here's a short story to explain.

I asked my son to clean the garage before going out with his friends. He agreed, went out to the garage, and was back in the house getting ready to meet his buddies only ten minutes later.

I went out to the garage. Well, it was a bit tidier than it had been before Alex did his work, but it didn't meet my expectation of a clean garage.

When I asked Alex to clean the garage, I didn't assign a time frame to it, so he was free to use his (teenager's) discretion. I should have asked him to "take thirty minutes and clean the garage." The amount of time I suggested would have been enough for Alex to understand how clean I expected the garage would be when he was done—sports equipment stowed where it belonged, tools back on their hooks, trash thrown away, and the floor swept.

Apply Parkinson's Law. When you assign a task, give an estimated time to complete it. You'll get the job done the way you expect. You'll also prevent overachievers from spending too much time on a given task. If you ask an employee to clean the front windows—in your mind, a twenty-minute job—and four hours later she's still at it, you'll wish you had suggested a time frame.

Make your communication clearer and improve your employees' productivity. It's the law.

Do the numbers for meetings.

90 – MINUTES IS the maximum time a department managers' meeting should last. Any longer, and it's a retreat, not a meeting!

75 – percent of meeting time should be spent on topics about the future. No more than one quarter of a meeting should be spent discussing last week.

60 – minutes is the minimum duration for most meetings. Plan your meeting carefully and don't shortchange your discussions.

25 – percent of time the meeting's leader should talk. Don't let the store manager dominate the conversation. Keep all the participants engaged.

8 – topics *at most* on the agenda. Too many topics make for a messy meeting. All the topics discussed should be important to everyone in the meeting. If there are topics that involve only a few managers, discuss them at another time. Eight topics at ten

minutes per topic will keep the meeting within the 90-minute maximum length, too.

5 – minutes to summarize at the end of the meeting: "*Who* will do *what* by *when*?" Ask a participant to summarize the meeting. Rotate the responsibility by selecting a name out of a hat at the end of the meeting. That will encourage everyone to pay close attention and take detailed notes during the meeting.

2 – employees (non-managers) can be invited to join the department managers' meeting. Including one full-timer and one part-timer, rotated weekly, gives associates the opportunity to learn more about how the store is managed, and managers the opportunity to have access to associates' opinions. You might even spark interest among some associates in becoming management candidates.

1 – department managers' meeting per week. No more, no less!

Hire better.

WHEN AN EMPLOYEE leaves your company, it's a huge inconvenience and a huge expense. According to the US Department of Labor and the Food Marketing Institute, the cost of turnover of one employee ranges from $5,000 to $10,000.

One of the best ways to reduce employee turnover is to hire better. Here are four steps to improve your interviewing process, which will help you hire employees who are right for the job:

1. When a new candidate first asks for an application, have the highest-ranking manager available at that time conduct a three-minute interview. The manager asks three questions:

- "Why are you applying with us?" ... to determine if the candidate has a sincere desire to work for *your* company.

- "Why do we offer paper or plastic bags?" ... to evaluate the candidate's understanding of customer service.

- "What is the price of our ten-pound bag of Idaho potatoes?" ... to see if the candidate tries to make up an answer or shows honesty by admitting he/she doesn't know.

2. Interview the candidate three times before offering a position. One of those interviews should be given by a pair of potential co-workers.

   At Whole Foods, associates participate in the interview process. When employees are involved in hiring decisions, they work hard to make sure the person they helped choose succeeds.

3. Do at least three reference checks on every candidate before hiring. Even if the previous employer doesn't give much specific information, you can learn a lot from the tone of voice and what's *not* said about your candidate.

4. Give final say to the manager of the department where the new hire will start work. The manager who owns the decision will be

more committed to the success of the new employee.

And a successful new employee equals . . . less turnover!

Provide a fair chance to succeed.

A NEW EMPLOYEE deserves a fair chance to succeed in the new job—a fair amount of time and personal attention.

Let's start with time.

By a show of hands with many audiences, I've determined the average number of hours allocated to the orientation of a new employee, part-time or full, is a meager eight.

With only eight hours of orientation, a new employee is being thrown into the deep end with only the hope he can swim. Imagine a soldier with eight hours of training going to battle with one who had forty hours. It would likely be a short war.

Some of the best retailers commit a minimum of

twenty and some allocate up to forty hours to give their new hires a thorough orientation to the company and the job.

Now, let's talk about the attention paid to new employees.

On that first day, the employee's first twenty minutes on the job should be spent with the store manager. That's the employee's role model, and it makes sense for the first exposure to be to the leader of the whole store. *Never* start a new employee on the store manager's day off.

Here's what the best retailers do with their longer hours of employee orientation:

- More shadowing of trained staff
- More role-playing to get comfortable dealing with various situations
- More testing and certifying to ensure new employees know how to perform their duties
- More fun activities like scavenger hunts to build teamwork

Give your new employees a fair chance to succeed. It will be worth the extra time spent.

Assess employee attitude.

I OFTEN HEAR, "We follow our employee turnover rate closely and know we have a problem when that rate begins to rise." But that's closing the barn door after the horse has escaped! It's far wiser to measure your employees' mood *before* they think about leaving.

That's what an employee attitude survey is designed to do. This can be a ten-question informal survey taken in the break room or a thirty-five question survey anonymously completed online. Whatever survey technique you choose, checking your employees' mood on a regular basis can add tremendous insight into how happy your team is

on the job. Employees who dislike their jobs won't be engaged at work or offer outstanding customer service.

Assess your employee's attitudes regularly and professionally at least once every two years.

Monitoring your employees' mood is so crucial, I recommend basing at least twenty percent of the store manager's bonus on the results of the employee attitude surveys. A store manager who increases employees' positive attitudes toward the company and their jobs is worth more than a product-focused store manager who lives only for a tight inventory and low shrink. That manager's employees are probably missing out on a proper orientation, adequate recognition, and a professionally administered performance review.

Put your aces in their places.

YOUR VERY BEST associates—your "aces"—should be working during the busiest hours and in the positions that maximize their talents.

Supermarket operators often give their best employees the earlier shifts to get their departments set up properly in the morning. Unfortunately, by doing this, your best employees clock out by 4:00 p.m., about one hour before the bulk of your business arrives.

List the ten employees you consider your absolute best—your aces—including full-time and part-time employees. Write their daily schedules, by day and by the hour. Then write your store's busiest days and hours. Compare your store's busiest times to when your aces are on duty. Are your best employees there when you really need them?

Store and department managers should also be in the store when it's busiest—at minimum, two nights per week to 6:30 p.m. and one night per month until closing (overnight in a 24-hour store).

Don't force dramatic changes in your key associates' schedules. Instead, slowly rework their schedules over a three- to four-week period and explain why the changes are necessary. Let them know that they are your aces and that your store's potential can only be achieved if they are in the most important places on the schedule.

Give 'em a life.

POST YOUR EMPLOYEES' schedules by 5:00 p.m. on Wednesday for the upcoming week. When you don't give employees a few days' notice of their schedules, you put unnecessary strain on their personal lives. How can they make plans for a family outing or a doctor's appointment when their work week (starting Sunday) is not revealed until the preceding Friday or Saturday?

Be prepared that the earlier a schedule is posted, the more likely employees will request changes. But the inconvenience of a few schedule changes or employee substitutions is nothing compared to subjecting your entire staff to the stress of posting their schedules on short notice.

Give 'em more control of their personal life. They deserve it and you can do it.

Maintain discipline.

MOST EMPLOYEES WILL break a company rule at some point. But it's what happens *after* the infraction that matters most.

If a swift verbal action is taken to coach the employee on the correct procedure, chances are the infraction will be an isolated incident. If another infraction occurs, a more serious action must be taken. Your disciplinary process should move from verbal coaching to a verbal reprimand in the office, then to a formal write-up, and then a suspension.

Make sure all employees know your disciplinary process, and that they know you will use it when it's needed. Good employees don't want to watch co-workers underperform without repercussions.

Many people fondly remember their toughest teacher as one of their favorites. Consistent use of a well-designed disciplinary process will help you

coach a poor performer into a desirable associate over time and earn a reputation of holding people accountable for their actions.

Break the break room blues.

ALL GOOD BREAK rooms have the basics: a clean sink, table and chairs, clean restrooms, and employee lockers nearby. On the walls: an updated bulletin board, a large poster of the company's mission statement, and photos/short bios of all the managers in the store.

Great break rooms have the basics, but lots more. Here are some ideas:

- Employee photos from the last promotional event

- Announcements of current promotions

- Updated chart showing the store's progress towards its "items sold per customer" goal

- Photos/bios of new associates
- Basket of complimentary fresh fruit
- Book and magazine exchange
- Large flat-screen TV
- and even . . . a Nintendo or Xbox gaming system

Top-notch retailers understand the correlation between employees who feel appreciated and increased sales figures. A clean, comfortable, and entertaining break room demonstrates clearly to employees that management knows they are important to the company.

It's no surprise that Publix Supermarkets' break rooms are first class. The company is a perennial in the *Fortune* "100 Best Companies to Work For" list.

Make sure your break room tells employees, "We appreciate you—enjoy your break!"

Listen to your customers.

YOU WANT TO know what your customers think about your store—the good, the bad, and the ugly. To get an accurate picture, use at least three different ways to get customer feedback.

1. Interact with customers one-to-one on the sales floor.

Many store managers rely on comments that they hear directly from the "horse's mouth." But this allows for a very limited sample size. Only the squeaky wheels speak up; the non-confrontational types will simply leave after being disappointed, never to return.

2. Solicit feedback in quieter ways.

Print an invitation to give online feedback on the receipt, or place a suggestion box at customer service or at the exit. Make sure you have signage to encourage customers to drop their comments in the box.

3. Get formal feedback through focus groups or in-store interviews.

You can target specific customer groups (new, older, teenagers) with pre-determined questions. This is more proactive than waiting for a suggestion to be dropped in the box. Dorothy Lane Markets in Ohio has effectively used a customer advisory council for many years. The council meets quarterly to guide management toward better decisions.

And one more reminder: be open to customer complaints. You don't need to hear what you're doing well—solicit feedback to help you make changes that will improve your store's operation. Listen to your customers!

Know your enemy.

IN WAR AND in business, from the ancient Chinese military strategist Sun Tzu, know your enemy.

It's key in supermarket retailing, too. Knowing your competitors' strengths and weaknesses is very valuable when allocating your own resources.

Knowing your enemy means more than studying their ads. Conduct a one-day trading area assessment twice a year. Put together a team of store and department managers and visit three or four stores for thirty to sixty minutes each.

Require everyone on the team to find at least one good, usable idea in each store. This will force the group to look closely at the stores. These ideas can be

discussed in future manager meetings and strategic planning sessions.

Stew Leonard's in Connecticut and New York has been famous for their trips in and outside their trading area. Their policy forbids any manager in the team to talk about the negatives they see in a competitor's store. Their rationale: you can't improve by looking at what your competition is doing poorly, so why waste the time? Look for ideas that they do better than you, and think about how your store can adopt them.

Know your enemy . . . and use what you learn to *your* advantage.

Work as a clerk.

EVERY SUPERMARKET EXECUTIVE and store manager should work as a clerk on a regular basis. It's a great way to find areas that need improvement.

Each month, work four to five consecutive hours as a clerk in one department. Uniform, name tag, and all. Choose a different department every month. Put yourself under the complete control of the department manager to assign your work. Don't take calls or interrupt your shift for any reason.

Employees will love seeing a manager or executive trying to do the work they do. They will appreciate that their bosses are making a sincere effort to understand their roles. And the customers who shop there while you work as a clerk will find out who you are and be impressed by your level of commitment.

After each session of working as a clerk, document the improvements you think could be made in that department. Never criticize or second-guess any employee or manager while working. Wait a day or two to discuss possible improvements with the department manager.

I worked as a clerk early in my supermarket career when my stepfather brought me into management directly out of graduate school. I knew nothing about the day-to-day tasks in a supermarket, and I used this method to learn what makes it work—or not work.

Stay grounded. Make time every month to work as a clerk.

NOTE 1

At least three charities will benefit from your purchase of this book. The publisher and I worked hard to minimize the production costs. I pledge to contribute all proceeds (after costs of production are paid) to help children, help animals in need, and feed the hungry. Thanks for assisting us in this endeavor.

NOTE 2

I would be grateful for your opinion on any of these rules. If you'd like to, please send me (harold@hlloydpresents.com) a rule of yours that could (or should) be added to the list. The supermarket business is a tough one, and we can all learn from each other.

Enjoy the journey!

Also by Harold C. Lloyd

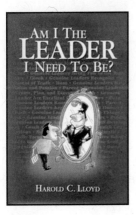

Am I the Leader I Need to Be?, a book and DVD by Harold C. Lloyd, will help you find the Genuine Leader within you. Through discussion, examples, illustrations, exhortations, and exercises, this book will help improve your Leadership Quotient (LQ), a measurement crucial to your success.

$19.95
ISBN: 0-97-11542-5-2
190 pp.

We all know we waste time at work, but most of us don't know how much. Author Harold C. Lloyd shows us how to reclaim at least five hours each week by using the ideas in his book, *It's About Time*.

$19.95
ISBN: 978-0-9711542-9-2
166 pp.

Available at
www.brigantinemedia.com